I0158494

We surmise our being in the content perceived by our audience, when, in actuality, it is a tiny portion of our true make-up and our aptitude. The author chose to move beyond this plain into the vast universe. She chose to welcome magnificence, to dream of a conquest that is everlasting, ever powerful and ever...

This book is dedicated to my beautiful son. You have taught me the most important lesson in life. There is incredible strength in our love.

Pinki Pandey

SHATTERED INNOCENCE

Memoirs of an Indian Woman

AUSTIN MACAULEY PUBLISHERS™
LONDON • CAMBRIDGE • NEW YORK • SHARJAH

Ordering Information:
Quantity sales: special discounts are available on quantity purchases by corporations, associations, and others. For details, contact the publisher at the address below.

Publisher's Cataloging-in-Publication data
Pandey, Pinki
Shattered Innocence: Memoirs of an Indian Woman

ISBN 9781643786421 (Paperback)
ISBN 9781643786438 (Hardback)
ISBN 9781645368427 (ePub e-book)

Library of Congress Control Number: 2019907761

The main category of the book — POETRY / Subjects & Themes / Family

www.austinmacauley.com/us

First Published (2019)
Austin Macauley Publishers LLC
40 Wall Street, 28th Floor
New York, NY 10005
USA
mail-usa@austinmacauley.com
+1(646)5125767

I would like to extend my sincerest gratitude to all my family and friends who propelled me with their positivity to evolve and transform into the strong woman I am today.

Table of Contents

1
Introduction

She sat in the corner of the room, curled up into a tight ball. Her hands were shaking with fear, and her head was foggy from all the tears she had shed. Unable to weep any longer, she remained silent to the world, trying desperately to push out that morning blowup with him.

She could recollect every detail, from the flopping of his arms in rage, to the curses he spewed from his mouth. He looked at her as if she was vile filth, and she returned his look with innocence, unable to comprehend how her accidental breaking of a glass in the new sink or the spilling of orange juice over an expensive marble island had anything to do with her self-worth.

There was an eerie satisfaction he got each time he exploded on her. He expunged a massive load of weight he secretly carried in his cerebral cortex. It was Pandora's box full of awful childhood memories that replayed through every fight.

Yet as unbelievable as it sounded to her, slowly but surely the toxicity crept into her lungs, compressing the air around her. She was profoundly impacted with his relentless scrutiny of her human flaws, normal to most people but despicable to him. These very natural imperfections became so visible to her, and made her question every moral fiber in her make-up.

She repeated her name over and over. Mizra used to glide smoothly from the tip of her tongue. Now it weighed heavily, like dead weight. This prompted her to try others. She called her father's name a few times, very softly, and ended up chanting *Ohm* several times. She prayed one day soon she could relinquish the pain where the scars resided, embedded deeply into the tiniest crevices of her body. Maybe this was why she ached both emotionally and physically. Exhaustion had taken its course. Restful sleep was a scarcity. Nightmares would frequently travel her dreams and combust into pieces, waking her up with startles or sharp screams, with tears rolling down her eyes.

She stretched for a mirror nearby and held it uneasily, anxious of what she would see. Peering at herself with uncertainty was not the easiest feeling. She felt herself fleeting with each outburst, so she focused on gravitating back into herself and searching deeply for that familiarity in her eyes. Ever so slowly her pupils appeared to glimmer with the softness she was fond of. Signing with relief, she hugged herself tightly.

What lay in front of her was a pen and a notebook. Mizra stared at them intently, certain she could channel the energy into words. Her fingers were one of the few things that he could not extinguish. The live content poured out of her like strong currents. It was how the language flowed onto the paper, when her speech failed her, that allowed her safe passage and offered a self-therapy outlet. Her fragile fingers fumbled clumsily, as the script rushed out from its barriers.

In the very moment of when I thought I had become a defeatist, my sweet son found me like he always did, just at the brink of time, as if he knew I needed that thrust from the bottomless marsh pit.

He galloped to my side like a baby colt would. "Mama, Mama! Come play with me! I love you!" His eyes shimmered with glimmer and his face sparkled with a glorious ray of sunshine.

The color that faded rushed back into my soul, rejuvenating me with hope and fueling me with determination. You see, just hanging on was a success. For each day I lived, I loved more. I grew stronger. I fueled my faith with my stamina and my resilience. We all have to journey to that dark place in order to stare at it in the face, pay our respect, and walk away from the ugliness with confidence.

When you read this book, I hope you are able to see a journey embedded with infinite discoveries about myself and the people who surround me, both good and bad. I hope you can see that even in the weakest of my moments, when I was at my lowest point, I was able to muster up courage. My poems and my memoirs are as sweet with joy and laughter as they are infused with pain and agony. I am a Fighter, and thankfully I am a Survivor.

There were times I was petrified, worried sick to my stomach I would not see another day. I lost so much weight because I could not keep anything down. I am sure, to many people I looked frail. But to the ones that stood close to me throughout the turmoil, they knew the truth. They knew my fierceness was immeasurable. They knew I had endured a heavy burden that normally would crumble others. They knew the size of my heart was equally as massive as my determination. They saw the depth in my fortitude when I could not. And they made sure to tell me that over and over again. For their endless support, I will always be grateful. Their love and empathy leaves me speechless to this day. Humanity and kindness exist, and will find us when we least expect it to.

2

Angels Looking Over Her

It is in that one incredible moment, an epiphany, where one realizes that Miraculous Women have walked the same journey before you, and there will be many more after you. I thank my dear girlfriend, Amanda Diamond, for being that angel for me.

She gently whispered in her tiny ear
You will not break, stand strong my sweet dear
As you shower head to toe in your infinite tears
Trickle down, those unsavory fears.

This too, like others, shall pass
That knot in your stomach, that tight mass
Those tiny spasms, let them rush through your fragile nerves
Let them flush.

You are strong, harness your strength
Measure how far you have gone each day, its length
However big, however small
Move forward, angel, despite each painful fall.

So much pure love is in your heart
Do not ever let the humanity part
The suffering will slowly reside
So will the hurt you secretly hide

Listen to the silence; let it fill your heart
Let it softly resonate through each body part
To bring forth a new day where you stand tall
After all it's what comes naturally after a slow crawl
Your body will survive, your mind will heal
It is your soul; it is the one thing they cannot steal.

3
Today I Noticed the Vivid Green

Every one of those swirls can be transformed into tiny journeys within this very moment. You do not have to understand it. It is not within your grasp now, but it will be very soon. This is your body and mind telling you some big change is right around the corner. Just watch and listen.

Today I noticed the vivid green
Sparkling in the sun on the trees
The rays of sunshine amidst at work
Unveiling the cloud over my head that lurked
Tip toe, waddle waddle, bump thump
You prance playfully next to me.

Taking the grainy sand in your hand
And with your bare feet digging into the bare land
All the while smiling endlessly so innocently
And giggling, heehee hoohoo haahaa.

Everything you do is so natural and graceful
Every touch is genuine at heart
Breathing each experience into your lungs
Only exhaling once you've soaked it in
All the while showing me how
Easy it is to be you as it is to be me.

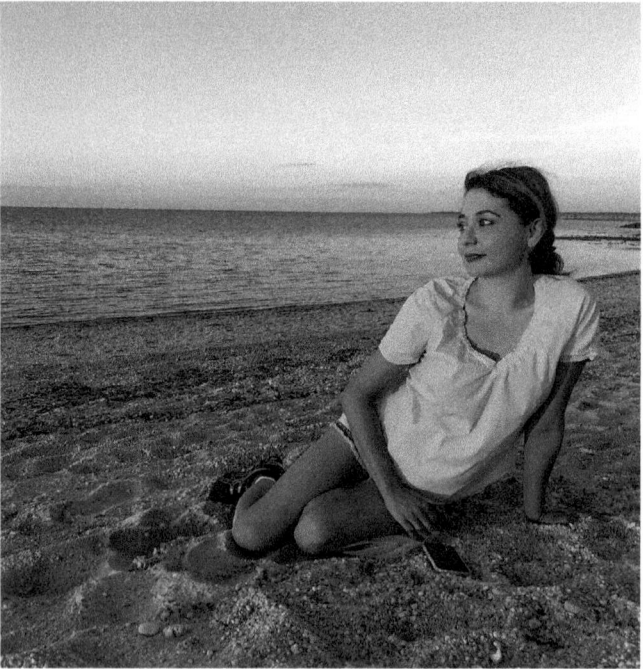

4

Music in Your Heart

He took her under his roof
Then blew around her a museum surrounded with single
shards
Laying before her skillfully a deck of cards
Claiming to hold her future in one hand
And the ground beneath her was his property, not her land.

My dearest, My only child
Have forgiveness in those that do us wrong
Their lips project an inaudible song
Their vision blurred and their speech slurred.

They know not what they are so they search
Awaiting to sting the next as they perch
In search of qualities they lack
In the hopes of stealing it back
Whether they never had it, or lost along the way
They are so messed up inside, so they cannot really say.

Look beyond them and into your own soul
They can pretend they know you,
But it is plain lies because they are not whole

There is a music in your heart
It beats so loudly, it calls so proudly
The beauty is it is wild, yet so very mild
Its manners, its gestures are not through lectures.
It is a freedom, a blast, a surge
That resonates in others, a holy purge
It signifies the immeasurable
The Sun, the Stars, the Cosmic Universe
They all live within You
My Love, my Light, so true.

5

The Bucket You Hold

Most of us are taught to pick ourselves up as a child. It is the same throughout the entire journey of our life. The more of what we acquire is what we are surrounded by. Some have a huge supply of love pouring in through the windows. Others have a medley mix tossed into a huge salad bowl through a limited window. Regardless, as an adult, you chose where you decide to reside. My home resides in my heart. This is for my son, as he continues to teach me more every day and every year that passes as he gets older. I love you, my sweet boy!

I love the world for all the little things that sometimes one forgets about

For the life that grows outside

From the trees that dance in the wind as they are grounded firmly in the dirt

As the leaves whistle, shoveling in the bushel

From the birds that remain in the midst of an awakening thunder

Perching together high up top on one branch right next to each other

As they sing their farewell song, stretching miles beyond very long, full of wonder

Saying I love you just like you have done so for your child

Now lay down your arms and let your heart be mild

For a better beginning, for each day is a new start

And the bucket you hold is what you have chosen to live in your heart.

6

I Am the Storm

He grabbed my arm and I clenched my teeth, biting my lower lip to distract myself. His mouth opened up like jaws to spew vile filth. I lost count how many times this happened. He was always angry at me. I could not stand still enough, nor talk fast enough. My movements were not fast enough. My delivery was not swift enough. Everything about me seemed to bother him.

Instead, my thoughts were in momentum to a natural stride. My impression carried a glorious pride. To be alive and move forward, despite the ditches I had accidentally fallen into was a success. So I stared back at him in silence, secretly building a layer of resilience and openly exerting a fierce stamina that would alert my spirit each time he tried to diminish my being. I had taken an incredible lift, larger than actual physical mass. It is called "Abuse," and I was engulfed in its domain daily. It would change me in ways I could not comprehend at the time. The Abuse would swallow me whole, only to spit me out in entirety.

"The devil whispered in her ear, You will not survive this storm. She whispered back – I Am the Storm

7
The Right Man

The right man will protect you
He will shield you, yet teach you to be strong
He will embrace every part of you as the universe welcomes change
He will hold the banner for you at the finish line, rooting for you the whole way.

The right woman will guide you
She will talk to you gently and give you a deeper perspective
That goodness stems from within oneself
And from this develops a strength that is immeasurable and displayed in our every action
That what we take must be given back to the world
And in return you will find a devout purpose of belonging to something bigger and sweeter.

The right man will recognize and salute such a woman
Put her on a pedestal for all these reasons and even more
Because she is the vessel of new life

To a child that will evolve even beyond her own magnificence.

8
Orange

Orange is his favorite color, he tells me
It is a medley of the deepest parts of the bottomless sea
From fluorescent coral reefs to indecent flashlight fish
Which he has only seen in pictures
And yet still his heart must miss
That he longs to befriend the spider crab
And the giant tube worm
Saying I should follow him with courage and a conviction
that is firm
So I do
We swim beside the 16-feet sixgill shark
Then hold its fin as it glides through the murky dark
All along at play in its very own park
With scattered rainforest kelp leaves afloat
Glistening as the sun hits their glossy coat.

Then we bump into stingrays that lay camouflaged on the
seafloor
Waiting for that moment we step into their door
To a secret entrance that brings infinitely more
Of all the glorious creatures that simply glide and soar.

Then we plunge into deep discovery dives
To find most beautiful plants in the deepest of the hives
Their colors exude a glorious array
Of such luminosity I could not even say.

First comes the red sea whip
With tentacles resting peacefully, daring you to dip
Then comes the sea anemone
And around it the clown fish swim
In clusters around the tropical reef rim
Then comes the plumose anemone
So pearly white as it grows three feet high
With a furry pouf on top, its sting-like rays let us easily by
Only to land into a plain of all sorts of different sea grass
From turtle to manatee to shoal
Such a colorful wonder makes you feel truly whole.

Where's the Orange I ask him?
It's in my heart
There's no rhythm in its rhyme
There's no beat as sublime
It's just what you feel
It's me, I'm the key to your heart
I broke the secret seal.

9
You Are a Fighter,
Just Like Me

He softly titled her head up with one hand, so that she would have to look at him. With the other hand he ever-so-gently caught the tears dripping down her face. She felt so weak, exhausted from the arduous climb. She felt like she was being sucked into quicksand, and no matter what she did, this life was swallowing her whole. She was scared that one day the pain would engulf her. She had to find more strength somewhere within her; if not for herself, then for the very child she loved more than anything.

He took her hands firmly within his, squeezing them tightly. "You feel this?" he asked. She nodded. "You aren't numb. Your body, your mind, and your soul are elevating to a higher realm than where you are at now. People evolve most when they are compressed, or driven to survive. Your beauty is your resilience, your courage, and your compassion. You will make it through this fierce storm. You are a fighter just like me, just much smaller."

She looked at him in awe, unable to answer. He returned her gaze steadily.

10
The Law Guardian

She stared at her client coldly. She was the law guardian and held a lot of clout in the system. She made huge differences in people's lives, whether positive or negative. By now she had lost her objectivity and compassion. She had seen too many of us, one too many times.

The system processed us in mass quantity and depreciated our value, our story, and the struggle we experienced. To her, I was simply another face, but to me she was my hope. The problem was I did not know where to start, because the entire journey was embedded with pain. I was beaten down. I knew that I needed to convey my message delicately yet firmly, because that is what mothers should do. As quickly as I began to pour out my story was as quickly as she shut me out.

Judgment had consumed her daily course, as objectivity was buried deeper with every case. She had no kids. She had no attachments that could ground her in such a strong current. She shielded her heart for protection, so she had no compassion left for me. How could she ever know that my journey was just as hard as hers? How could she relate to the plight of an undermined, battered woman? It was not that she could not. It was that she chose not to.

11
Agility

Agility is the secret ingredient to growth and will allow you to transform though swirls and curls. It will guide you through dark tunnels in a manner that is profoundly intrinsic to one's inner courage, to explore and make surprising discoveries throughout our journey. It will lay way to flexibility and adaptation when constant change is inevitable.

Your thoughts are inherently subjective, especially when you are in close proximity to the situation. Stand back several feet and reassess from more of a distance. Apply reasoning to the components, and you will see that, in most cases, at the face of fear lies evolution.

Then, at that very moment, you have embraced all of yourself, understanding something hugely important. That learning and overcoming is not finite. It is a constant momentum.

12
My Journey

Hurting does not last forever
Your mind is clever and it knows better
It is the heart that decides to rest, dormant to shield itself
from the torment.

Waiting patiently for that something or that someone to
uncover
A fiery storm with sparks of thunder
A sparkling breeze full of chill and wonder
A blazing plain where a beautiful dame
Ponders a better route, a less crowded lane.

And when to awaken to trust her instincts
Challenge her limitations
Question her perception
Trace back from completion to conception.

What it took for her to climb such a feat
And the strength it took to ride the beast
That expanded her vision where she dared envision
A world that is what she makes it.

13

Pure Love and Forgiveness

One day you will be ready to stop punishing yourself. One day you will be ready to embrace all of you. One day you will realize you are the sum of your accumulative experiences. Our mistakes are the core components to a holistic journey, where both trials and tribunes intricately wave your colorful being.

This very day you will be able to look at others and apply true empathy and consideration. You will be able to discard the harsh judgment which binds them in the same manner it did to you. Society's social norms were created to provide governance. Do not allow these boundaries to restrict and define your being. You have exceeded society's restricted views. You have elevated yourself to a higher realm. At your core is pure love and forgiveness. At the core of society is uniformity.

14
Black

Black is the medley, a silly mixture so deadly
It is when you take a rainbow with every color
Some totally vivid and others duller
And ever so gently smush them very finely together
Taking super delicately a pregnant ostrich's plucked
feather
Swirling them, then swishing them
Accompanied by a friend named Ben
Who repeats the motion squirting on it more lotion
Alyssa has got to sit and pray which is the ultimate
ingredient of the potion
Chanting the letters LOVE
While Jaylin releases the gentle DOVE
And then they all link hands and say:
For All of Us to Get Along,
We have to believe that Together We Belong.

15
My Beloved Mother

I remember when I was young and unafraid
With you by my side while in bed I laid
The air smelled fresh and the grass looked green
Everything was familiar and so very serene.

Yes, those were the days in each picture display
The sun shines down on us its glorious rays
A sense of youth as a child is what you gave
That is what I carry in my heart and save.

I remember when I was young and had no fear
You were my mother and I was your baby dear
You in my life is all that I knew
Imagining any other way seemed so impossible to be true.

And now I must face my biggest quest
To take a different role in life is the ultimate test
With you no longer in the lead
I am scared that I will not succeed.

But I guarantee you I will not fail
With the strength of your love, we will prevail
Beloved Mother, take my hand in your very own
This journey we will take together; you will not be alone.

I will be your armor through the treacherous ride
Believe me when I say I will never leave your side
I will provide courage when you are weak
Draw from within me the strength you seek.

As you are the child of God, I am the child of you
The days of awakening nears, but think not the sky's blue
Please hear this much…
      You are a miracle that God has given me
      So precious no other gift can ever be
      I would never turn around and change a thing
      These words to you I loudly sing.

16
I Am Writing Again

We grow out of necessity
We love out of desire
We expand to avoid combustion
We learn from our failures
We bruise from falling
We move forward by picking ourselves up.

Here I am standing
And every time landing
With both of my feet grounded
Because from within, at the center
What I choose to reside has become my mentor… LOVE

"Dear God, may the bright Spirit keep the child in me
alive ALWAYS and forever!"

17
Sometimes My Faith Waivers

To my one and only true love, my precious son.

Sometimes my faith wavers
All of my doubt creeps up
I question if I am good enough
If I'm being punished for all my mistakes and all my sins.

And I yearn to be free
It is at that moment that I realize I am enslaved by my own demons
They follow me everywhere, reminding me of how flawed I am.

I can't remember when I started feeling this way, imperfect
I simply scrutinize each one of my presence and my actions
Wondering if I will ever stop and just forgive myself
Then I stare into your eyes and see bits and pieces of myself.

Yet better and more whole, kinder and innocent
My anger, frustration, and confusion subside
And give way to hope for a future that is filled with happiness.

I pray for so much more for you
The things you see should be brighter
And your spectrum of vision should be broader
You should allow yourself to understand you are human.

Your journey will consist of ups and downs
Falling is an important lesson, because it will humble you
It will remind you to continue to satiate your thirst
In life it is the trials and tribunes that will define you
Just hold strong and be true to yourself
Understand that fear is in courage
Know that happiness is not without pain.

I will always stand behind you, watching you from close by
I will protect you, shielding you as much as I'm capable
I will travel to the end of the galaxy and back
Just to put a smile on your precious face.

Goodbye apathy, Hello love
Goodbye hatred; welcome a profound understanding
That the world holds pockets of goodness, and you and I are it
I will face my regrets
Look at them in the eye one last time and repeat a mantra every day.

I will begin today, moving forward

I will lay the groundwork, creating a soundboard beneath our feet

The cure is in the palm of my hands

Faith, trust, and belief pulse throughout my veins and stem from my heart

Wisdom is understanding we project our reflection onto others

So I will love myself and shower you with this sweet goodness.

18

Appreciation for the Simple Stuff

For my Prince

Sometimes life is about hard choices

It is about not giving up on the people you feel least deserve it

It is about surfing the waves without sinking

It is about realizing your purpose in life is complex

It is about conquering your foe by accepting them with grace

It is about discarding baggage, simply because the guilt is too heavy to bare

It is about diffusing a fight before it results in a fabric tear.

When your life does not make sense, it is exactly where you should be

To piece together parts of yourself you lost along the way

Hold your ground, stand strong

And as scary as it may be, face the storm

Your tears shed will cleanse this old soul.

Then you will start seeing what is really inside
An avid determination to fight
A profound wisdom from your mistakes
Forgiveness for those who stood in your way
Credit to them for making you strong
An endless love for those who stood by you
And a well-earned profound respect for yourself
An enhanced vision to see the forest among the trees
An incredible appreciation for the simple stuff.

At the beach

19
You Are Not Alone

This one is for my family, such kindred and special souls. It is in the moment of darkness where the isolation leaves you bare and even more aware. Your journey is simply an approximation of a series of circles, at the heart of which lies a truth. This truth is that you are not alone in this medley mix.

There was a time I cared for everyone, where I wanted to overcome hurdles

But I realize in my latter years that I have made transformations in investing my time in the right people

The ones that cared enough about me, that wanted to dig through all my complicated layers equally, turned out to be my biggest supporters and in return, me their biggest fan

Life is about taking risks and diving into a medley mix

It is about getting in the deep trenches and walking through fire

It is about teaching yourself to strive for higher

For the cause that will get you closer to a simple yet complex truth

Love, passion, curiosity, and hunger is the motivating element

The design will always be confusing, and the uncertainty equally disturbing

But if you want to find the answers, challenge and elevate yourself

There really is no other way but to live on the edge

Plunge into it headfirst, pouring your heart, soul, and mind

And in the end, you will come full circle to find the value you left behind

Happiness is imbedded in all the great things we nourish our sweet soul with

It is more than the successes of work

It is the pitter-patter of your child's feet on the doorsteps

Awaiting anxiously the moment that is best

When they open their arms wide for you to embrace them by your side

In the darkness there is a light

Running around and around as you fight

And as the questions tear you inside

Stripping you until you have nothing left to hide

Brilliancy is understanding you know nothing yet feel everything

Silently with each emotion and each fall until at last you are able to stand tall

Proud of what you've become, after all the miles you've run

To only come back to what's real

Life in its worst and finest moments will heal and rejuvenate the hearts that beat

To, in time, find the right persons are in your very audience seat.

20
Depression

She tippy toed downstairs only to hear muffled whimpers. His tears were silent, and fell to the wayside in plight. The depression ran deep, with a depth that was hard to assess its true origin. He spoke nothing about it, only expressed it through explosions of anger on me. The magnitude of this presence had grown since we first met, cultivating with each layer of barrier he put up to ward himself from the world and from life. He could not easily partake in laughter as I did. I felt the joy slip through his fingers with every feeble attempt, dissolving slowly and painfully before his eyes. He held the letter in his weak hands. The letter would implode the little logic and sanity he desperately clung to. He would soon plunge into anarchy, a realm void of governance, boundaries, and respect.

21

Mama, I'm Following You Too

Sometimes the journey of a child isn't always easy
Normal things like skipping and jumping can make them queasy
Running from point A to point B makes them wheezy
Things that seem easy become difficult
Like clasping a pencil in the same manner
And coloring a logo on a banner
Or balancing still for seconds on one leg and then another
As he awkwardly fumbles to grab his mother.

Sometimes, it is this very child that intellectually excels
Ringing and jiggling all your alarms and bells
Counting and reading for the simple thirst of curiosity
Hoping in return for a genuine kindness and generosity.

Sometimes, it this very child in gym class that fell
Bursting with excitement and sprouting emotionally to tell
A story that is so simple yet so deep
A world full of people that are different yet the same
Where variances aren't to blame
They are all a part of life, all a part of the game.

And every now and then you will see it more
In someone next to you, at the core
Just like the weather and the winter chills
The balance is what the hot summer fills
That there is beauty in the sun that feeds the earth with its
glorious ray
Just as there is in the moon which hums you to sleep until
the next day.

Sometimes this very child teaches you unconditional love
without limits
Or boundaries because there is no fear
When you've opened your heart to someone who is that
special and dear.

That through thick and thin means a journey
Full of twist and unexpected turns
And strength and faith is what you'll learn
Will carry you through the most painful of night
When you just can't see the damn light.

Sometimes, it is this very child that draws you closer to
humanity
When the world has its fill of insanity
Giving you the courage and will to succeed
To continue multiplying every good deed.

As this little boy watches, tip toeing behind
Hoping there is meaning in it that he will find
Then one day he looks up to you
And says, "Mama, I am following you too."

Our hearts intertwined

22
The Test

The mother that cried for you, cried because she had been there. The father that left you saying he loved you, is because he wanted that love to surround you when he was gone. The brother that had insight to see there was a fierce beast in you did so because he has the same fiery core. The sister that promised you that your heart would remain whole did so because she too grieved and survived to tell the story with a punch.

The friend that told you you are strong did so because he lived through that dark age only to have journeyed past the storm. The friend that told you are an angel has the same value that she extends forward about herself. The friend that asks you for help does so because she will pay it back by moving forward in life. The others that survived the arduous climb know you will too. These are the very energies that will rejuvenate your soul, too. We gravitate to them the most when our heart seeks sustenance. And we find each other again and again to validate a truth within our grasp. We find people our body needs, whether to supplement or test our faith.

23
The Enchantress

From out of nowhere materialized an enchantress, who had whitish purple hair and a dress that was light pink. She was very tall, as tall as a basketball player hovering around us tiny people. The fabric of her dress was woven from silk, embroidered with different-colored beads in the shape of flowers. There were subtle glimpses of blue, yellow, and green that shifted shades of their true color as she moved. It was like nothing I had ever seen. Her voluptuous lips were a glossy pink, far surpassing the kind you only see in pictures of famous actresses which men lust after. Her skin had a glossy silvery glow, and carried quite a bit of sparkle to it against the sunlight.

Butterflies and all sorts of birds fluttered around her, singing aloud as if her presence enhanced their very existence. She touched them all with the pure love she emanated. She held her head high as she glided towards us in a composed manner, walking with an elegance that mandated both reverence and dignity. Her beauty was like a soft and gentle spring sunrise. My manners temporarily failed to register, and I gawked at this magnificent being in admiration. Then suddenly I was staring back at myself in the mirror until I blinked, and the vision was almost gone, still faintly glimmering with light. And I knew right then what it was. For a moment I saw a flash of the potential aptitude I had within my heart, surpassing all the limitations, as the power crystallized into the palms of my precious hands.

It was my writing…

24
Hope

She glanced at her watch in disbelief. It is as if time had frozen and she was stuck in the warp. She watched the judge's lips as it moved in slow motion. The divorce was final, and so was the onslaught of endless, brutal swipes and attacks from him. The judge wished the frail women lighter and happier days, because she had known and seen how much she endured. The tears just started to stream down her face, literally forming a puddle on the table, unable to hold back the flood of emotions she purposefully withheld in order to sustain her stamina and fierce determination to survive. The only thing that held her together was the thought of her son being without her gentle touch. So she forcefully walked tiny steps forward regardless of how difficult as it was every day, or how heavy her feet felt.

She endured three years of pain, which was exceedingly too long even for characters in a movie. Everyone in the audience looked at her with sympathy, finally acknowledging how arduous the journey was on her, finally seeing her as a human being rather than a number. Everyone turned to watch her as she wept with both happiness and sadness. She was squashed to a pulp, the compression so unbearable at times she would gag or heave.

She lost 18 pounds since the onset of the divorce to now, which her petite frame could not afford to lose. She was 95 pounds and five feet. It made her terribly weak until her body was entirely drained. The poor thing became numb, building layers to shield her delicate heart that lay petrified at the core. Her heart screamed for help every day, as silently she whimpered under her breath.

And it was at that very moment the Judge, her attorney, and the child attorney hopefully searched her eyes for a tiny source of flare left in her. She couldn't show them it was still there, hiding away in the very far corner, frightened of being misread and taken advantage of again. She knew better. This journey had nearly killed her. She stared at them blankly while the tears kept rolling off her checks and chin as if there was a strong downward current.

She had fallen several times, grasping for the very air that surrounded her. He tried to forcefully talk to her, as if he had ownership over her, not that he ever deserved her. She coldly ignored him, diluting his presence to a mist left over from a hot stormy night. He had willfully ripped into her ego and torn it to shreds. The damage ran deep, and there were ruptures all throughout her where her soul bled to excrete the toxins.

Her attorney leaned over gently. "It's over. You made it! I'm so proud of you. I'm honored to have you as my client." She stared back shockingly at Hope. It was still alive and present, even if it came in small quantities, even if it was outnumbered. It was out there seeking its way to desperate women like her.

25

My Sister

I looked at the bottle of pills and assessed the potential damage it could do to me. I still remained in the same clothes in my new apartment which was unexpectedly bare, lying on the bare floor with just a sheet over me. My friend gave it to me out of kindness.

Leaving my son even if it meant temporarily tore my heart. I wailed profusely in my barren new apartment, screaming at times for the Spirits and God to hear me. Then I took the bottle and threw it across the room. As my spirit dwindled, so did my energy. I fell asleep into a deep state only to hear the phone ringing over and over again, nonstop. Whomever it was on the other end was relentless. Daylight crept in from the windows as it did into my sub-consciousness.

I fumbled to pick up the phone. On the other end was my sister; a fierce, compassionate, and beautiful Amazon lady. She was not tame; so very few dared to challenge her.

"Don't you give up, baby! Don't you ever think I'm not around! I have your back! What you endured is incomprehensive and implacable, and disgusting. This makes you the strongest person I know!"

So I sobbed profusely, as she broke down with me, for me. She knew how difficult it was for her little sister to stay afloat. She would never let me go, and she made sure that it was known.

Faith is knowing people will come to you just at the right moments, even when you feel the darkness swallowing you whole. There is a glimmer in the darkness that you cannot see. It is this very glimmer that awaits to lift you up from the hellish pit. I don't know what this entity is. All I know is the light called to me when I needed it the most.

26
Women Shall Stand Together

Mizra stood on the sidelines, watching her son dance with his school friends at the Valentine's dance. He was such a happy kid and she wanted to keep it that way. To see him so curious and full of love, life, and laughter was what sustained her. The kids held hands as they spun in a circle, and then followed each move that was instructed by the DJ. Inside there was such a complexity of emotions running through her veins. The divorce had just begun, and she was frightened. She had no family and barely any friends here.

From the corner of her eye, Mizra noticed one of the mothers. This very mother walked over to her, smiling. They started chatting, and instantly both felt the warmth and uncanny connection. Then by the grace of Lord, this mother said something Mizra would never forget.

"You seem like you'd be the perfect best friend."

Secretly, Mizra needed someone like her too. "I'd love it if I could be your friend!"

Since that very moment, each of them infused faith and hope into each other, knowing their bond was not coincidental. They both had their own stories, and silently would align to display true partnership, founded on acceptance and love.

This world is what we can make of it together, united. I shall always be thankful for the kind and strong women in my life. I would not have made it through without them.

27
Behind Locked Doors

I crawled into bed, laying my head in between my knees. I pulled the covers over myself, creeping out a tiny opening. His feet paced back and forth in front of the guest bedroom, where I was staying. My heart raced so fast it felt like it was going to pop out of my chest. I had gotten the lock changed. It needed a key to open it from the outside. You would think that would stop him, but it didn't. I could feel his rage swell up, as he turned the knob left and right multiple times banging on the door.

I laid to my side, shaking and watching as he paced in front of the door. I took his control away by pulling away from him. I wanted to be free of the toxicity. His world was slowly imploding in his plain sight.

I had asked life for more. I knew this life I lived was a contortion of the true vast variety. I knew, most importantly, that if I stayed my son would put us on the podium as the one major relationship to reflect on, and likely unconsciously mimic it. And I would never let that happen. He was better, so much more than I could hope for. I closed my eyes and pictured my son in front of me a ways ahead, and walked forward to him. I picked him up, as I always did, and kept walking into the light. That is how I fell asleep that night and every night afterward.

28
Thanks to My Son,
My Inspiration

By My Son

Adamant is the rarest jewel. Our car is made from quartz. You can only find quartz in the Underworld. We are from the Overworld. And here is a science fact. Adamant is rarer than quartz. Adamant is extremely rare and found in caves both in Netherlands and Overworld. It is rarer than Vibranium which is from Wakanda.

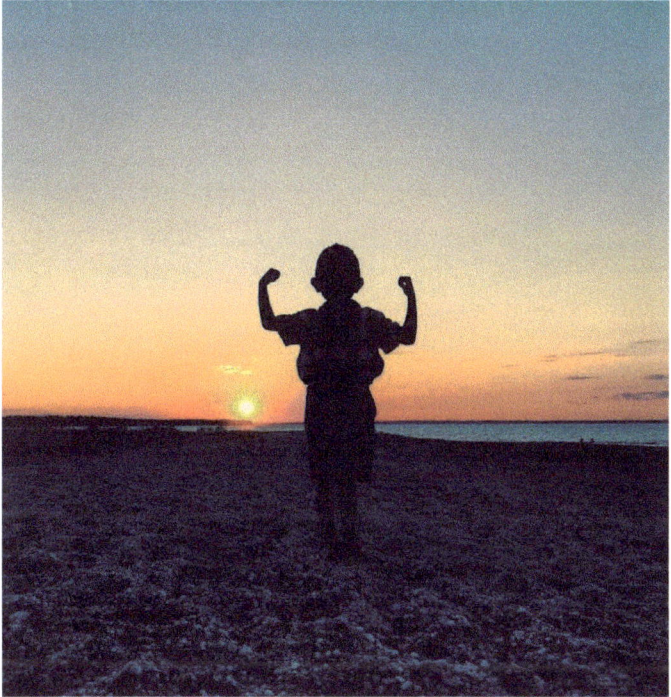

Strength is not reflective of size. It lies within your heart.